GREAT TO FOLLOW

By David G. Guerra

•

Fiction

Doughboy City

Air Bridge Berlin

Spandau Guard

Non-Fiction

The Walking Leader

GREAT TO FOLLOW

The 20 Rules To Becoming A Better Follower And
A Leader That's Great To Follow
By David G. Guerra

David G. Guerra

GREAT TO FOLLOW (The 20 Rules To Becoming A Better Follower And A Leader That's Great To Follow)

Subject headings:

Non-Fiction – Business – Leadership
Non-Fiction – Self-Help – Professional Development
Non-Fiction – Self-Help – Personal Growth

ISBN: 1508625948
ISBN-13: 978-1508625940

website: http://www.daveguerra.com/books/GTF

blog: daveguerra.blogspot.com

email: dave@daveguerra.com

Cover design by David G. Guerra.

First Printing: 2015
10 9 8 7 6 5 4 3 2 1

Table of Contents

Acknowledgments

Introduction

Rule #1 You Know Nothing!

Rule #2 Know Your Role

Rule #3 Expect To Be Held Accountable

Rule #4 Ask Questions

Rule #5 Get To Know The Good Veterans

Rule #6 Watch Out For The Cranky Old Timers

Rule #7 Continue Your Education

Rule #8 Get A Mentor

Rule #9 You Are Who You Hang Out With

Rule #10 Stay Visible

Rule #11 Volunteer But Don't Look Like You Are Volunteering

Rule #12 Demand The Best From Your Superiors

Rule #13 You Are Not A Spy

Rule #14 Take That Extra Step

Rule #15 Know Your Co-Workers

Rule #16 Share With Others

Rule #17 Evaluate Yourself, Constantly

Rule #18 Bring More To The Company Buffet Than Just Your Appetite

Rule #19 Be Patient

Rule #20 Have Fun!

Rule #21 (Bonus) Work Is To Stay At Work & Home Is To Stay At Home

References

Acknowledgments

The biggest thanks go to Teresa (my wife), Emma and Matthew (my children), Luci (my mother), Martin & Barbara (my in-laws), Joel, Jorge, & Juan (my brothers), the rest of my family and all my dear friends. I will never be able to tell you just how much your support has meant and continues to mean to me.

Another big Thanks goes to those that served with U.S. Army Berlin Command and Berlin Brigade (1945-1994). It is an honor to have served and be associated with such great Soldiers, Airmen, and Leaders.

Thank You,

David G. Guerra

Introduction

GREAT TO FOLLOW

It has been written to be a Leader that is Great To Follow one has to be an even greater follower. I truly believe this. There have been numerous times that I have been a follower whether I liked it or not. Now with all my experience, by no means do I claim to be a leader, let alone a great leader. Quite the opposite, in fact I am a lifelong follower. I follow all the Leaders I have encountered. Unfortunately, there have been bad managers that truly believed they were great leaders and that belief would eventually become their undoing. Always, those individuals failed to recognize what bad management is and only perpetuate bad management by doing what they do to the next generation of employees. The undoing of some people I encountered in my military and civilian life was so overwhelming that I would not even come close to considering them leaders, to begin with. Sure, they had positions of authority but that did not make them "automatic" leaders. Expected or automatic leadership is a misnomer as Leadership has to be earned and is NEVER just given. The expectation of "given" leadership is usually accompanied by a promotion for sticking around long enough or getting a diploma or degree or because they own the company. These are the wrong reasons for giving or putting someone in a leadership position.

There have been many Great Leaders and a few bad managers in my life. Luckily, there have been more good Leaders than bad ones. Unfortunately, there were people like my Platoon Sergeant at my first duty assignment or my section chief at my last duty assignment; in civilian life, there was a recent graduate of a prominent Texas agricultural and mechanical university, and a small red head with a Napoléon complex. I may be a little harsh in my description but each of these four individuals certainly had it coming. Each one was a in a position of authority and each one had a problem being the kind of individual I would follow to hell and back. Oh sure, each one of them made me a better person and showed me I did not have to follow them or emulate their behavior to be successful, they clearly showed me if I wanted to be a great manager and leader of men and women I must never do what they did. Unfortunately, somewhere along the way, these four individuals were fed misinformation and believed if their job title put them in a position that required individuals to report to them, then they were automatically "leaders". Nothing could be further from the truth.

However, on more than one occasion, to their employees, these four were egotistic, ego-centric, individuals who when it came down to it could not lead a cub scout troop out of a jungle gym. Now do not get me wrong, these individuals worked hard to get to where they were when our paths converged and parted ways. They were not "gifted" their positions of management. They worked hard to climb the ranks of their organization except for the one who graduated college and filled a "management trainee" position. Most of them took the normal path to management while one was on the accelerated route. Now, I am not going to make this a book that bashes these four individuals. I will use them as examples of where and how I learned from them and why their actions must be a future cautionary tale.

As I wrote, in my time in the military and civilian life, I have encountered many Great Leaders and of course, many more individuals that had greatness in them but out of fear or self-preservation decided that to act as the leaders they wanted to be would mean the end of their careers. Then again, a few never knew they were allowed to be great. That is why I wrote the Walking Leader. Someone had to let them know greatness was within their grasp and most importantly, you need NO ONE'S permission to be Great!

I know in time, some of those individuals will break out, go beyond their self-imposed chains, and achieve the GREATNESS they desire to achieve. Who knows maybe one day I will break through as well. However, in the meantime, here we are, on the precipice of Greatness but we have so far to go and so much to learn and know.

This manuscript should serve as another guide from me to you. This time let us look at it from the Frontlines on up the chain of command or up the organizational chart. This time you and I are in the trenches, together! We will talk about what it takes to be a

Great Follower first then a Great Leader with or without anyone's permission or approval. On this journey, we will meet the good, the bad and the uncertain. Lastly, I have changed the names of the guilty and the innocent, however, the deeds are all their own.

Rule #1
You Know Nothing!

When it comes to starting any new job or filling a new position there is one thing you should fully grasp and know without fail: **YOU KNOW NOTHING!**

By knowing nothing, I mean you are a green as the day is long. Sure you completed Basic Training or Vocational School or College or Graduate School but you know nothing about the real world you are about to enter. Unless you have worked in the real world before or while going to school you have absolutely no clue as to the mess you are capable of making or how deep the mud you are about to step into really is. Very few training or academic organizations have any inclination as to what the real world is all about for their graduates. Sure, they offer their students access to case studies and you are afforded an opportunity to subscribe to your chosen vocation's professional journal but all of that is sterile and detached.

In most cases, the information is so old it is of little to no value to the student.

Then comes where you will work, with the exception of the U.S. Armed Forces, no other organization guarantees you job placement after your schooling. After signing up for a two, three or four year hitch the Armed Forces sends you to an eight to thirteen week "Basic Training" before you even see your first job at a base or ship somewhere on the planet. In the Public and Private Sectors, you are expected to have the minimum education and skills requirements met before you even think of setting foot in the Human Resources Department. Stick with me, here is where the "you know nothing" part comes in. You might know how to do your job but I can all but guarantee you do not know how your employer wants it done. If you have never worked for your current organization before this job then you also know nothing about the corporate culture other than the 'well-groomed' public facing side you and the rest of the world have seen, know, and understand.

The need for every organization, no matter the size, to have at least a two week to at most a one-month orientation course whose sole purpose is to ensure that EVERY new hire learns, understands, and lives the organization's "way of doing business" culture is of the utmost priority. Unfortunately, due to the almost always need of "boots" on the ground, small businesses might be able to commit two or three days to get the new hires up to speed. If you find yourself in the latter situation then immediately assume the role of a sponge and soak it all in.

My first experience with an "orientation course" was when I arrived, after Basic & AIT, to my assignment with the United States Army Berlin Brigade in (then) West Berlin. As part of "in-processing" with the Berlin Brigade, I signed up to attend the Berlin Brigade School of Standards (SOS). It was at this "school" that all new arrivals learned what it was like to be assigned to one of the most unique units of the US Army in one of the most unique cities in the world.

Here are a few of the things we learned and had to understand:

- Our Role In the Occupied City of Berlin
- Status of Forces Agreement (SOFA)
- US Forces in Berlin / Ambassadors of the USA

- How to travel to and from East Berlin (ONLY)
- Proximity of Soviet Forces
- Status of the East German Government and Military Forces
- Off Limits Areas
- 2 weeks of Introductory German

The School of Standards was not limited to only enlisted soldiers newly assigned to the Berlin Brigade but to ALL new members assigned to the unit. This meant everyone from the lowliest private to the Commanding General attended the two-week course. This "shotgun approach" ensured EVERYONE received the same information about what the Berlin Brigade was, what it meant to be in Berlin, what the expectations of a soldier assigned to the Berlin Brigade were, and what to expect if those expectations were NOT met.

Trust me, I never knew what the meaning of "persona non grata" truly meant until I was told in no uncertain terms what it was and how it could apply to me or any other soldier in Berlin or Germany or any country other than the United States. I was set for my entire time in West Berlin and experienced as much as I could while

9

performing my duty as a Berlin Brigade Soldier was expected to perform that duty. Of course, there were some that failed to meet the standards and as promised, they were quickly shown the way out of the divided city. I left the city the normal way. I was assigned to a new unit after completing my assigned duration (two years) in Berlin. Unfortunately, my next duty station did not have a "School of Standards" and it showed.

The culture at my stateside assignment was laid back, the sense of urgency and level of Professionalism was not at the high level that I had grown accustomed to in Berlin. There was a sense of teamwork but not at the level and depth of commitment, I had the honor of experiencing 110 miles behind the Iron Curtain. I am not knocking soldiers at any stateside Army base but those who served at an overseas duty assignment first felt the same culture shock I did. Then again, it was both a little gratifying and scary of the culture shock those young soldiers would have being 110 miles behind the Iron Curtain after having experienced a stateside assignment first. They had no clue what was in store for them. Luckily, the Berlin Brigade's school of standards or orientation course existed to help them with their transition to the new duty assignment. It helped make life a little easier as everyone had the same information to make their stay in the divided city a successful one.

Organizations that can dedicate time, resources, and committed staff to train all new hires in the corporate culture are the organizations that are going places. Smaller organizations might not have the luxury of time or resources to dedicate days or weeks to the training of the new hires and should not stop them from doing what has got to be done. What the small company can do is continually train the new hire about the corporate culture and corporate expectations of all new hires at every opportunity that arises. That is the only way you are truly going to fit into your role within the organization. Otherwise, your role might turn out to be of the "guy who worked here for a couple of days." Ideally, you want to know what your role is as quickly as possible unless the mission or the situation dictates otherwise.

Rule #2
Know Your Role

I have been and done many things over my military and civilian careers. I was an Infantryman, a College Student, a Network Analyst, Department Head, and Operations Manager. However, one thing is the same among all those titles: at the start of each job, I knew I had a place in the hierarchy and that place was at the bottom of the organization chart or being low man on the Totem Pole. That is right; I did not start any of my jobs as the "Head Honcho" or the "Big Cheese". Far from it. I guess it comes from being the child of a career Army soldier. You learn rank structure quickly in the military. As a military family member, you learn everything has a place and an order to it.

For example, if my brothers or I did something wrong on base, we usually did not get in trouble from the MPs or the Base command. Oh no, that was reserved for my father. The next morning he would be called to his

Commander's office and get his backside chewed off. He was responsible for us and our actions. When our actions violated base policy and procedure, my father was the one that was called on it. In the military and in the corporate world there is an old saying "poop rolls downhill and you do not want to be at the bottom of the hill" (and poop is not the word that is most often used). After the commander finished with my father, guess who was at the bottom of the hill? It was not pleasant. It never is pleasant being at the bottom of the hill. However, that is the price you pay for being the new guy in an organization or the children of a soldier that lives on a military base (remember: bottom of the totem pole).

That is exactly the way it is in any organization when a "newbie" arrives with a few exceptions. First, everyone knows you are going to make mistakes. Second, most everyone knows you will not learn from your mistakes until those mistakes start to affect or are on the verge of affecting your pocketbook. Fortunately, for my brothers and me, we learned by living on a military base, for every one of our actions there were reactions. By the time we left the house, we knew we were the masters of our fate. Whatever path in life my brothers and I chose to take was made that much easier by clearly knowing our role.

Every company has positions that must be filled. Typically, the first ones to get filled are the best positions (as viewed from the bottom up) like Chief Executive Officer, Chief Finance Officer, and Vice President of Operations. You get what I mean. Those people are usually the founders, friends of the founder, or heaven forbid, a family member of the company founder. Unless you are the founder or a friend of the founder, you probably are not going to be starting at the top of the corporate ladder. That is perfectly all right. Someone has to be the big chief, head honcho, or the HMFIC just like there has to be the person that fills orders, sweeps and mops the floors, or answers the phone for the CEO. That is the way the corporate ladder is built, wide rungs at the bottom that get very narrow as you get closer to the top. Did I mention the rungs get very narrow at the top? If the top of the ladder, the corporate ladder, is your final destination within the organization then you must fully understand that unless your mother is the CEO, you are NOT going to skyrocket to the top of the corporate ladder on your first week of employment.

As someone starting out with a new company in an entry-level position, and whether you have more schooling or more work experience than the guy or gal you report to, you have to remember one thing and only thing: **KNOW YOUR ROLE!**

What I mean by know your role is KNOW EXACTLY WHAT YOU WERE HIRED TO DO. Know exactly what you are expected to do. Know exactly where you fit in within the organization. Then and only then can you really see how the organizational chart is laid out. However, do not just know what your job in the company is. Do not just know where you are in the organization chart. Do not just know that in the grand scheme of things you know nothing. Do not just know all of that but understand all of it, completely and thoroughly understand all of it!

Early on in your career and while you are getting to know your role you might become frustrated. Frustrated in how the organization does things. Frustrated in the fact that you think you know a better way of running the company and you are ready to storm into the CEO's office to give that "joker" a piece of your mind. Is that really a good idea? Most certainly, everyone, including me, has thought about giving the "top dog" a piece of their mind. However, it is not prudent nor will it make you stay with the company for very long. You might find in the end, the only person that knows nothing may be you in that you suddenly find yourself without a job. Take the time to know the company, what it really does, the people (your co-workers) and what they really do, and of course, work to fit in to the corporate culture. With a little luck, you might find out just how much you do not know before you go storming into the boss' office.

Remember, the company culture has been around for quite a while. John Coleman in the Harvard Business Review wrote, "[t]here are other factors that influence culture. However, these six components can provide a firm foundation for shaping a new organization's culture. And identifying and understanding them more fully in an existing organization can be the first step to revitalizing or reshaping culture in a company looking for change." (Coleman, 2013) The six components he mentions are Vision, Values, Practices, People, Narrative, and Place and all of them were put into place long before you joined the company's payroll. One thing to remember, corporate cultures like every other culture is dynamic. That means it is always evolving, always changing. When any culture ceases to evolve, it means all its members are dead. When a corporate culture has stopped growing and evolving it means the end of the business side of the organization's operations as well as the end of its revenue-generating life cycle.

I understand it might take a long time for you to get a full grasp of the reality that is the enterprise you work for, however, you have to give it a chance before you can even think about changing the way they do things around here. Do not for one-second think you are the only person who has come up with the idea of making the place better or think that you know more than everyone else in the organization does. There have been plenty before you and there will be plenty after you, I guarantee it. Stick around long enough and one day the new kid will think he can do your job better than you can, so do not sweat it.

First, just get to know your place and your role. If you were hired to be an IT Support Tech then ONLY worry about being the best IT Support Tech the company has ever seen. Do not worry about what the guy or gal upstairs or down the hall is doing. They got there by doing something right and you will get there by doing something right, as well. You will most certainly get there if believe in yourself and have complete trust in your leadership and mentors (more on that later).

In the meantime, I am hereby formally advising you to keep your head down, put your shoulders into your work, keep moving forward, and keep your eyes and ears open, and please, please, please (don't make me beg) keep your mouth closed. Ignore this advice, if you choose to but you will almost instantly see where that will get you. Take this advice and make it yours, while you might not see where that will get you today, tomorrow, next week or next month but I can guarantee that before you know it you will see positive results.

Rule #3
Expect To Be Held Accountable

One thing has not changed since the first shepherd hired an associate shepherd to help drive the flock: no one is going to hire you and not check up on you. You should expect to be held accountable 100% of the time you work for someone else. No matter if you are making minimum wage or top dollar, you will be watched, always. They are watching to make sure they are getting a return on their investment. YOU. They are watching to ensure you fit in. That you can walk your talk. Do not be surprised when those that are watching you say something when you get caught doing anything wrong or not the way it is supposed to be done. Expect it. Now, if no one says anything to you when you know you have done something wrong or not done the company way then I would be highly suspect of the organization's true intentions and leadership.

Most organizations will hold you accountable, the sooner the better. If you expect not to be held accountable then you truly do not expect to stay with any organization for any length of time. As a businessperson, I would not hire an individual who does not expect to be held accountable. In this or any economy there is no time for waste and not holding people accountable means that waste is not the only thing that is happening with the company. When money is difficult to make or bring in which means one of two things is happening with the company: someone is stealing from the company without the boss knowing about it or worse that individual is stealing from the company because the boss is NOT holding anyone accountable.

Do not be fooled if you think no one is going to hold you accountable or no one is watching. As I wrote, someone is always watching and someone is always watching YOU. You are hired to fill a position and to do a job and in doing that job you expect to be paid. There is nothing wrong with that, what is wrong is when you are paid for not doing your job and you know you are not working the job you were hired to do. Once you are found out (you will be found out, count on it) what do you think will happen?

What will happen will be either you get counseled, put on notice, and held to a higher level of accountability or more than likely you will hear those two magical words, "You're Fired!" No one wants to hear those words; no one wants to have the boss hounding them to do their job. Then do not do what will get you in a situation that will garner their attention! Before you start to try to scam the system: DON'T!

Remember, you were selected from numerous candidates, you gave them a great interview, and the company did not hire you to sit around and do nothing for something. The only person who gets that position is the CEO's kid. Unless, your father is the CEO of the company do not even for a minute think you are going to get away with not being held accountable.

Look to the recent and not so recent past at what happened to ENRON, MCI/WORLDCOM, Bernard Lawrence "Bernie" Madoff, AIG, and every organization that needed a Federal bailout because of bad home loans. They were all, eventually, found out. There were legal problems and in the end, all of them had to pay. Even one man, Madoff, is paying right now. Because of the Ponzi scheme Madoff was given the maximum sentence of 150 years in federal prison. He will never see freedom in his lifetime and as of January 2015, Bernie Madoff is 76 years of age. Each of these organizations and individuals thought they were going to get away without being held accountable. Either they intimidated their employees not to say anything or they kept their actions to themselves. It was when individuals were out their money and had nothing to show for their investment or were extended credit when none should have been extended did the bottom fall out. They were found out only when it was too late. They worked hard to accumulate the clients and contracts they did but the not-so-funny thing is they worked even harder to not be discovered. All that time, effort, and money wasted.

There is something to be said about anyone who accepts being held accountable. That something is akin to words like promotable, up-and-comer, upwardly mobile, hot shot, and rock star to name a few. However, there are even more words for those that do not want to be held accountable: un-promotable, unmanageable, not a team player, thief, rogue, rebel, vagrant, unwelcome disruptor, and the list goes on and on. Now, there is only one of two paths to take when it comes to being held accountable. You can accept it as a normal function of the way the company does business or you can fight it and think you can do whatever you want to do and still get a paycheck (Yeah, Good Luck with that).

A word of advice: if you are looking for a job that is not going to hold you accountable then please keep looking because you are NOT ready to work in this economy and you are certainly NOT ready for a Big Boy / Big Girl Job. In the meantime, stick to shredding paper out at the warehouse or flipping burgers on the late shift. Even then, you will be held accountable.

Rule #4
Ask Questions

The only way to know is to ask! The only way to get something is to ask! The only way to move ahead is to ask! That is right, the only way you are going to learn how to do anything is to ask questions. Asking questions should be second nature for anyone in any business setting. It does not matter if you are a recent high school graduate or you have been working with a company since it first opened its doors, you must ask questions.

While all through your education you have asked questions, you probably asked so many questions that it drove your instructors batty. That is OK; they needed to be asked those questions to know what you know and to know how they were doing as instructors. However, there is something very unfortunate happens to many people after leaving school: they stop asking questions.

They stop asking questions as if by metamorphosis or magic beans they all of a sudden know everything and do not need to questions. This is when everything starts to go bad. The ego gets over inflated, and the common sense processers in the brain seem to all but shut down. People just stop asking questions and that is not a good thing.

Failing to ask questions will let other people think you got it under control. They will assume you know what to do, how to act, and you know how things are done around here until you go and do something to cause them to regret their assumptions. Never let people assume they know anything about you, never give them the opportunity to think you got it under control, especially if you are a very recent new hire. Do not try to pull the wool over anyone's eyes because you will be caught and when you do I guarantee there will be hell to pay. Please do not be offended but it is for your own good especially if no one has ever told you then let me be the first: YOU DON'T KNOW JACK!

As a new hire or anyone with less than a year under your belt with the organization it is safe to say YOU KNOW NOTHING (sound familiar?). I am not trying to insult your intelligence or belittle you. What I am trying to tell you is you have a long way to go before you fully understand the structure of the organization, how things are done and who is who in the organization. The only way to learn this and so much more is to ask questions.

You have no say in the matter you have no choice but to ASK QUESTIONS! Seriously, how else are you going to learn how to do your job? However, if you do have to ask questions about the basic function of your job then you might want to ask yourself if you can really do the job you were hired to do. A few other questions that are perfectly acceptable to ask should be those that deal directly with the corporate culture and how they do things around here. Certainly, ask about the special procedures in your job that are unique to the organization. Definitely, ask about the additional duties your job or your section/department/group may have.

I believe every conversation at work does not have to be about work. Therefore, it is acceptable to go ahead and ask questions that are not fundamental to the job you were hired to do. It is OK; just remember there is a time and place for everything. So pick the time wisely as to when to ask question that are not directly related to what you do or your section/department does.

Now the fine print: Ask too many questions and people will consider you a complete idiot. Yes, you have to remember not to ask too many questions. I know what you are thinking; first, I write that you have to ask questions then I turn around and write do not ask too many questions. Pick and choose the questions you ask. Make certain the line of questioning is moving in a positive direction. Then you stand a better chance of being called inquisitive. It is when you keep asking the same question over and over that people start to wonder whether you are the right person for the job. As a hiring supervisor, it took me a while for any employee I hired to overcome that stigma. Once the doubt starts to set in it is very difficult to change that negative to a positive.

Ask questions, ask plenty of questions but do not overdo it.

Rule #5
Get To Know The Good Veterans

No matter where you work, there will be two types of employees, the good ones and the not so good ones. To succeed with any organization it behooves all new employees to, as quickly as possible, identify who the good ones are and who are not. Doing this will greatly contribute to your success in the organization. On the other side of the coin, failing to distinguish the good from the bad, things will certainly not go the way you expect them. Whether this is your first job or your last there will be good and bad employees. Having good and bad employees is a good thing. I truly believe having both helps keep any organization on its toes. However, when the bad start to poison the entire operation things can turn for the worse. Unfortunate as it sounds, organizations do tolerate the bad employees. They can be tolerated for just so long.

Every organization also has "old-timers" otherwise known as the veterans. Those employees who have been with the company since "who flunk the chunk" are the veterans. They are the easiest to spot in the crowd, as they are usually the ones that are the crankiest. Maybe not all of them are cranky but rest assured those that appear to be the cranky ones are the ones that have been around a while. If there is anyone that has not been with the company for any length of time and is already cranky, one word of advice: RUN!

Back to the veterans of the organization. Just as it behooves you to identify who the good employees are it also behooves you to identify who the good long-term employees are. These veterans are the ones that know the company culture inside out, know how things really are done, and have a deep and extensive network of contacts within and without the organization. These individuals are the ones that are constantly building and rebuilding the company in the sense they have become the "go-to' people to get things done because they know what to do to get it done. Few people will go to the CEO or BRANCH DIRECTOR or FACILITY MANAGER when things need to be done. However, think about who they go to when they want it done right. They go to the veterans of the organization. Any leader worth his weight will seek out the advice of those veterans for at least two reasons: to find out how it was done in the past and to find out how it has been done wrong.

Those veterans will not pull any punches. Seriously, think about this. They have weathered countless storms and are still with the company. They are dedicated to the vision, mission, and leadership of the organization. They have also seen individuals come and go. They have become the de facto experts on who is going to make it in the company and who will be gone before they start. They might or might not have the educational background but they have the technical and streets smarts to make them priceless to the organization. You could say they really run the show.

These veterans are the ones that will also make or break you when it comes to your success within the company. They can help you down the path of greatness thus making your way up the corporate ladder a lot easier. On the other hand, they can heavily influence your lack of a future with the organization. By this I mean, the old timers have seen all kinds of people come and go within the organization that any upper level director or manager would be a fool not to seek out the advice and the wisdom of those veterans. Especially when it comes to getting feedback on the newbies, the up-and-comers, and the ones that are just there to collect a paycheck. Therefore, it is wise to go ahead and seek out those veterans, show them the respect they deserve, and find a way to learn from them.

Obviously, like anything you want to learn, especially from someone else, you will have to be patient. Remember, the good veterans have seen many "suck-ups", "fast movers", and those that are in it for the long haul during their tenure. They will be suspect of you and your intentions until they get to know you and which one of the three types you are. So let them get to know you, to get a feel for what you stand for, what you bring to the company buffet table, and what they see as you taking away from the organization. Trust them to see your intentions are nothing less than honorable. Once they make that connection, you are set. Again, believe that you are not to rush the process and do not do anything that will give any veteran, good or bad, any reason to believe you are not authentic in what you are trying to do and why you are doing it.

Rule #6
Watch Out For The Cranky Old Timers

At first glance, it may seem that avoiding the cranky old timers is easy to do but it is most difficult to accomplish. Every organization has at least one, two or more of these cranky old timers. That is OK, as every organization needs them. Then again there are organizations that one cranky old timer is one cranky old timer too many. Therefore, it is very important for anyone, not just followers but leaders as well to know how to identify them as quickly as possible. Once identified, it is becomes more important to know what to do with them and what not to do. Now do not get me wrong, you do not have to avoid all the cranky old timers but there are some that have resolved themselves to bring others down no matter what (please avoid them at all cost). Then again, others seem to just get by until they are forced into mandatory retirement. It is all about attitude with them and that is why you have to make your own decision early on.

It has been my experience that cranky old timers are needed and are important to the organization because they bring an unexpected, unique dose of reality to the workplace. I am by no means saying you should believe every cranky old-timer brings value to the organization. What I am trying to say or advocate is every organization should get rid of anyone that is not pulling their own weight, no matter how new or how long they have been with the company. There is no room for growth if there is one bad apple in the bunch. However, a reality is there will be a few individuals that management of the organization has recognized as needing to be let go a long time ago, yet they remain. These individuals will eventually catch on that either management has not done something to move them to a position that minimizes contact or better still remove them from the company payroll. As a new hire or an up and coming Rock Star in the organization, the sooner you learn to deal with such individuals the sooner you can skip past them anywhere you may encounter them.

Now, those "cranky old timers" that bring value are the ones that have been doing something right. Over time and for any number of reasons their attitude changed. They might absolutely love the job they do but are not happy with the company, the management, the practices, a staff member or whatever, yet they keep coming to work and keep banging out great value by giving their work ethic top priority. See not all cranky old-timers are bad for the organization. What is bad is their attitude and disdain towards the individuals they see as making them behave that way. They usually leave the new comers relatively alone however, should you seek them out be mindful.

While it is perfect to seek out all that is good in your organization, be careful. The good ones, the ones that have a beef with management or the leadership but deliver, are the ones that will take a while to get to know and get beyond their suspicion. However, once you get beyond their protective wall and are taken into their confidence be careful. Careful not be poisoned by their personal bias. It can happen but by being aware and on guard you should do just fine.

Get out there and get to know the good cranky old timers. Be careful not to fall into the trap a few of the cranky old-timers may have for you. They will set it and wait until the new guy or gal steps into it and next thing you know you are knee deep in it. They will do this to test your mettle.

Those old timers bring nothing to the organization but their negativity. Oh sure, a few of them have become old timers by doing the minimum that qualifies as "meets expectations" and not one bit more. It is very sad and unfortunately so very true. It is those old timers that do one thing very well and that is to poison the organization's culture by their words, deeds, and have no shame when it comes to spewing their venom on anyone and everyone. No one is immune to them. However, by identifying those individuals early on you can avoid or at least minimize the effects of the poison. Oh, I guarantee you will be bitten once or twice but do not fall into their trap and either bite back or worst still, join them.

Now, what happens if one of the cranky old timers happens to be your supervisor? You most certainly have an uphill battle ahead. However, do not feel all is lost. Quite the opposite, keep your chin up, tighten up your armor and get ready to go charging forward. You will most certainly have a rough road ahead. However, if your cranky old supervisor was present at the time of your interview(s) and was part of the final decision making to get you hired then consider that you must have done something right to impress even that cranky old-timer. So get out there, get to work, but be ready for almost anything. Most of all, when the cranky old timers are preparing to strike either walk softly and carry a big stick or take the path around them.

Rule #7
Continue Your Education

There is nothing better, in this world, than to have something no one can ever take away from you. That something is your education. All the knowledge and wisdom you acquire can never be returned. It cannot be refunded. It just cannot be taken away. There has not been invented (yet) a machine that can remove the knowledge and skills you have gained. That's right, what is in your mind can never be taken away or repossessed.

Knowing that, why would you not want to continue your education? The human brain might not appear to be big but it can hold quite a bit of information. According to Paul Reber, professor of psychology at Northwestern University, he declares the brain's memory storage capacity is "something closer to around 2.5 petabytes" (Reber, 2010). Breaking it down, it comes out to about 2.5 million gigabytes and that is quite a few flash drives. As you can see, you have plenty of room for more knowledge, experience, and memories so why not work hard to fill your mind? So seek out opportunities to continue your education.

Nothing shows your organization just how serious about your education and just how much of an asset you will be to the organization if you affirm and keep your commitment to continuing your education. Seeking and fulfilling your need to continuously self-improve is by far one large feather in your cap and says plenty about your character, integrity, and dedication.

By continuing your education, you also give yourself and every member in your organization an individual that has become open to new ideas and concepts. It is through experiencing the new ideas and concepts that you can bring something different and exciting to the organization. Based on those ideas and the unique application of them will fill the unique voids in your organization. It is not rocket science that I am talking about, unless you are a Rocket Scientist. I say that you are exposed to a new concept and you will be able to almost instantly recognize how your company can benefit from it.

You take it to the company and *POOF* you are a Rock Star! Obviously, it is not that simple but it could be.

Another aspect of continuing your education to consider is that of your legacy. The standard you set for yourself when it comes to education is the standard that others who follow you will have to emulate or exceed. Imagine your children and their children going further in their education than you did.

Now, imagine when it comes time to leave the company. Let us say, during your tenure you arrived with a High School Diploma, then you went to school and earned a bachelor's degree. You just upped the value of the position you are vacating. That in itself is not only a feather in your cap but in your organization's cap. Any organization would be crazy not to use your successfully earning a Bachelor's Degree as a hiring tool. In fact, more organizations are boasting the fact their employees have such degrees or certifications. It makes for a better-rounded and more open organization. Besides, it looks good on you as being one of the few who did instead of being one of the many who have not.

There is nothing wrong with not having a Bachelor's or Master's or a Ph.D. or a Certification. What is wrong is settling for the bare minimum and expecting to succeed. As the world has become an always on, 24/7 society you are always in competition with someone no matter where on the planet they are. You must understand the days of resting on your laurels because you think you have a job for life are long gone. Forget what your father and grandfather told you, the modern work place is evolving in that it promotes and rewards anyone that is willing to make the sacrifice, anyone that is willing to work the extra hour (no questions asked) and someone that believes; in order to be successful in the modern workplace means continuing your education. Failing any of that will find you at the back end of a very long unemployment line.

Is this a scare tactic? Yes and No! It is and I hope it helps motivate you to get off your duff and into the classroom (on your time). No one can make you get up from your chair at work and go to school or take a course. You have to do it yourself! It is not a scare tactic, in that I firmly believe real life should never be scary. However, what you should be scared of is becoming complacent and settling for the status quo. Once you become complacent the next thing you know you are being shown to the door with a plaque and small party to celebrate your retirement. Then what will you have to show up for it? Seriously, it serves you in the short term and in the long run to get in as much education as possible in order to show the organization you mean business but most importantly, to show yourself that you can do it.

Rule #8
Get A Mentor

In Rule #5 (Get To Know the Good Veterans) and Rule #6 (Watch out for the Cranky Old-Timers), I wrote about identifying the good veterans and the cranky old timers. By now, you should have a good idea as to how to pick the good eggs from the bad eggs. Therefore, the time is right to start hanging around the people who will help you advance within the organization. These individuals will be the ones that have no problem with it because they want to help others advance. In most cases, they have helped others advance, in the past, as well as advancing their own career. These individuals get it. They get the fact that by making life better for someone else they are making their own life better. So get out, find and hang out with someone. Remember you become whom you hang out with.

Just to be clear about what I mean when I say for you to hang out with others is to not go all stalker creepy on them. Start slow and steady. Be excited to be around them but do not appear to be overly excited to be around them. Be overly excited and it may get you a restraining order instead of an invite to an offsite working lunch. Follow their lead or simply listen and learn from them. Do not start forcing yourself on them instead of easing into the relationship. Be the student and they will be the teacher. After all, the objective of this relationship is to become a better employee thus becoming a better asset to the organization.

For any new relationship to blossom both parties have to see the mutual benefit of continuing the relationship. In this case, you want to progress within the organization and the other person wants to share her knowledge and wisdom of how she progressed and grew within the organization. Then consider it a match made in heaven. However, it is when one side of the relationship does not want to participate you should take that for what it is: nothing is going to grow. Then, it is time to move on.

In the case of getting a mentor, it may take you a while to find a suitable mentor or who knows you might find several people who want to mentor you. When you have numerous people wanting to mentor and lead you is when you know you are working with a great organization. We should all be so lucky. Unfortunately, not all organizations are loaded with people just waiting to mentor you and lead you down the path of individual and organizational greatness.

Again, remember to be patient. You have to be prepared to spend a lot of time meeting people, getting to know them and determining if they are willing to mentor you. Out of the individuals you identify as potential mentors, a few of them might not be up to having someone to mentor. They may be perfectly happy sharing with everyone, instead of just one, and it is perfectly all right. However, when the time comes it will all fall into place. Trust the process and it will deliver to you exactly what and whom you need.

Then in the future, you must remember to "pay it forward". Offer to help junior or senior people to create mentorship moments. It can only be viewed as a good thing. The best is to then make them recurring moments to learn and understand the context of the organization and how you could contribute to those issues." (Marcus,

2014)   This is a non-negotiable when it comes to mentoring. Someone took the time to mentor you, and then you must make the time to mentor others. For the sake of argument, let us make this rule #1 when it comes to mentoring.

A good piece of advice, when it comes time to finding someone to mentor, let them find you otherwise it may seem a little creepy. When the time is right, they will find you. The time may come sooner when you are the organization's "up and coming" Rock Star and it may take it a little longer for if you make yourself inaccessible to others. In the meantime, I ask that you trust the process and the person who needs a mentor will find you and it will be a perfect match. They are out there so do not sweat it and do not rush it. Be Patient.

Here is a little something else to consider. If by twist of fate the people you should be hanging around does not include your immediate supervisor do not worry. Your loyalty should always be to your immediate supervisor as she is who you report to, she is the one that is responsible for ensuring you are properly trained , he is the one who writes your performance review, she is held accountable for your actions whether she likes you or not. So do not lose sight of the fact that your boss is your boss and your boss does not have to be the mentor you are looking for. However, your boss, any good boss and every great boss should be a mentor by default.

Rule #9
You Are Who You Hang Out With

Someone once said you become just like the top five people you hang out with. If you have never heard this then let me tell you that statement is so very true. Not only is it accurate but you could say it is almost a scientific fact. Think about the following, back in high school when everyone was broken up by groups just as Grace did in "Ferris Bueller's Day Off", "the sportos, the motorheads, geeks, wastoids, dweebies", etc. Going into high school no one started out that way. OK maybe a few did but for the most part no one began high school that way. It was not until after everybody found their place or fell into place they became whom they hung out with. The JV football player hung out with other football players and thus he became part of the "sportos." The cheerleader hung out with just the cheerleaders so they became "the princesses". The members of the math club became "mathletes" and so on and so on.

You are not in high school anymore and now you have to pick a new team to play with, a new group of people to hang out with, and that means you will become just like them. Does this mean if you work in the accounting department that you will become just like everybody else in the accounting department? Yes. Just like those individuals who work in the maintenance department will be just like the other individuals in the maintenance department.

Why? Everyone wants to fit in; everyone wants to be part of the team, the Accounting Team. In all actuality, everyone wants to succeed and in order to succeed they have to become team players. Being a team player is the only way success in any organization will occur. No matter if it is for the company, the department, or for the individual everyone must play the game. It is understood, but I will say it anyway, you practice with the team (department or group) every day and you get better not just in doing the work but at becoming a fully integrated member of the team. However, being a fully integrated member of the team may come at a price.

The price is your attitude will reflect the type of people you are following. Follow good people and you have good attitude. On the opposite side, follow bad people and you know what your attitude is going to be! Now, you might not know you have a bad attitude because you are on the inside looking out. However, rest assured those that are on the outside looking in will see your bad attitude.

If you would like to move ahead in the organization, then stay away from those that have bad attitudes. Yes, it is that simple. Hang around people with good attitudes and before you know it, you will have a good attitude that others will see come shining through. If you are not too sure who has a good attitude and who does not then all you need to do is stop, look around you, and you will see who is who.

Usually those with a good attitude are the recognized leaders. They are the ones that people turn to in time of crisis. The people with a good attitude are ones that are grounded and deeply rooted in the organization. I say deeply rooted because they know what it takes to be with the organization for so long and they definitely know what it takes to move up within the organization. Find those people and you all but got it made.

Find the wrong people and I guarantee you this; you will not be long with the company. Once you have been identified as individual that hangs around with the "wrong people" then you can all but mark your calendar with the date of your departure. By this, I mean upper management is in no position to continually deal with bad eggs. The current economy and job market make it nonsense for any organization to put up with bad attitudes. Especially from those at the entry-level position. The organization's management and leadership wants to know their new hires are what they claimed to be on paper (job application & resume). Organizations want people who are dedicated and committed to making the organization the best it can possibly be.

In a 24/7 world, it means if the organization hires an individual that is not ready 100% to deliver on their stated promises of "I can do the job" they will not hesitate to replace you as you can rest assured there will always be somebody that can do the job you failed to do. Find yourself with a bad attitude and you will see "ain't no one got time for that." I know I cannot tell you who to hang out with and who not to hang out with but what I can tell you is a cold hard reality. The cold hard reality is those that hire you will expect you to make the right decision of whom you choose to "hang out" with at work and whom you "hang out" with outside of work.

Some choose wisely while others choose poorly. Be careful. There is nothing more I can say that has not already been said. You will know who the good crowd is and who the bad crowd is. You made it this far and you can make it all the way. Choose wisely.

Now, what if you do not hang out with anyone? Well, my friend the answer is perfectly clear. You hang out with no one then you become no one. If that sounds harsh than it should be because it was meant to be harsh. Unless you are a one-person operation, no one can do it alone. Unless everyone you work with is the wrong crowd that is the only exception. If everyone you work with goes against your moral fiber and integrity than it really is time for you to go and find a place that is more suited for you. I do understand there will be times you have to do what you do not want to do because you have obligations or commitments that cannot be broken. It is acceptable and understandable. However, what is not acceptable and not understandable is to be in a place that goes against who you are. Find a way out and do not look back.

Never forget and always remember the person that hired you is always watching you. Those individual(s) will want to know they are getting a suitable return on their investment. You are that investment. Choose wisely, because the decision you finally make might not be one that helps you succeed and grow within the organization.

Rule #10
Stay Visible

No matter how new you are or how long you have been with the organization there is one thing you have to remember: you must stay visible. Staying visible means you have to make certain those that supervise you can see you and know what you are doing. If you are like me, when I was starting out, I was micromanaged and I really hated to have someone standing over me and watching everything I was doing. It was as if I was not trusted.

Now, I understand being the new person means that no one really trusts you. They know what you were hired to do and they know what the expectation of the job is. However, what they do not know is you. In the case of the military, the noncommissioned officers and officers know what anyone straight from basic training is capable of doing. However, those new soldiers lack the experience and wisdom that comes with doing their job for longer than just the basic training period. Having been fresh from basic and assigned to a high profile unit as the Berlin Brigade meant there was a lot to learn and do right the first time. There was little room for error. It meant in order to learn to do what I had to do, I had to get out there and be visible.

A word of warning about being visible; be prepared to be "volunteered" when a volunteer is needed for a "special assignment". Do not worry about being "volunteered". It will pass as it did for me when the next new person arrived to the unit.

Of course, there will be times when a call for volunteers goes out in a unique fashion as it has been for many young privates. A Sergeant or other Non-Commissioned Officer would ask, "Who knows how to drive stick?" Then when some naïve young private would say he knows how to drive stick, the Sergeant would hand him a broom and tell him to drive the broomstick all along the dayroom floor.

Over time, remaining visible will be one of those things people will remember about you. Being visible will have its benefits. You stand a greater chance of being selected for extra assignments or sent to a conference or better still, sent to a training which will further your career within the organization. You may ask yourself why?

The answer is perfectly clear: the decision makers remember you. Those people see you as someone who chooses not to hide in their cubicle but wants to participate and be part of the organizational team.

Another word or two about being visible. Now, this is not all going to be just handed to you. You will most definitely have to work for it. By this I mean though, you may be visible what you do during that time will matter most. If you are goofing off, having a good time with everybody, and not really getting anything done, which would be a very bad thing. The same applies if you are just kissing ass. Well, the results are understood but I will say it anyway: that is not a good thing!

You have to stay focused doing your job, putting in the hours, paying your dues, and making stuff happen. No matter what your job is, do not lose track of what you must do today and every day. Yes, it may be necessary at times to blow off a little steam and goof off a bit but you and I both know the moment you even consider goofing off is the moment your boss will walk out of his office. Therefore, why not play it safe and save the goofing off for after work when you are expected to blow off steam.

Show your supervisor, your teammates, and your supervisor's supervisor you have nothing to hide, you know what you are doing, and you are not afraid to be seen doing your job.

Rule #11
Volunteer But Don't Look Like You Are Volunteering

One of the first things you learn when joining the Army is you never volunteer for anything. However, things happen and volunteers are needed. One day our Platoon Sergeant asked for a volunteer. No one was quick to volunteer. Not too happy with the response he asked again. Again, no one volunteered. By this point, our Platoon Sergeant was starting to get a bit perturbed and needed a volunteer, as it was obvious he did not want to volunteer someone. Just before asking for the third time the Platoon Sergeant informed us, "If I don't get a volunteer I will volunteer someone." Reluctantly, a hand came up from the back of the platoon formation. The Platoon Sergeant called the young Private to the front of the formation. The Private was told he was dismissed and to enjoy his day off. Stunned everyone else in the platoon was tasked to go to our training area and perform area maintenance and beautification. The next day, our Platoon Sergeant had another assignment that *required a volunteer, when he asked everyone raised their hand. Every time there after he had no problem getting volunteers.*

If there is one, other, thing I have learned from working in the Military, Public, and Private Sectors is there will always come a time when a call for volunteers will be made. I am not talking about volunteers to head off on dangerous mission or to fill sandbags to help prevent damage from rising river's flood. The kind of volunteer I am talking about is for an individual (or a small group) to do some task many would consider menial or a job no one wants to do. To be a bit clearer, I am talking about things like heading the annual fund raising event for your organization, to work on the weekend, or to rake the snow. That's right I said rake the snow.

In the military, especially for those living in the barracks there is something known as "area beautification" which I have always understood and known to be: mowing the lawn, trimming the hedges, sweeping the sidewalks, raking the leaves, and so on. However, one time an early snowfall came and coated the area with at least two inches of snow. The bad thing was there were still leaves on the trees. Well, a strong wind accompanied the snow and the leaves fell onto the fresh snow. Therefore, the powers that be called for the leaves to be removed. Needless, to say there we were for the first time in our young lives raking snow. In this situation, there was no call for volunteers as the CQ (ranking Non-Commissioned Officer in Charge) called for everyone that was in the barracks to get to work raking the snow (more appropriately raking the leaves off the snow).

If you have ever spent any time in the military or talked to anyone about their military experience the one thing almost everyone tells you or you know is to "never volunteer for anything". While there is some substance behind this great piece of advice there is also something very wrong about it. When it comes time to volunteer, most managers or supervisors ask for volunteers and then add "or be prepared to be volunteered" should no one step up. The thing is no one wants to volunteer anybody however, it is a task most managers detest it is also one they cannot avoid. Their superiors have given them a task and it must be completed either by volunteers or by those that were "volunteered", it does not matter it just has to be done.

As one of the people that is being supervised or managed by a person that has been tasked to ask for volunteers do not feel bad if you were chosen to be volunteered. The call for volunteers did go out and when no one volunteers then all bets are off. Of course, there will be individuals that will take it personally and it will lead to animosity, resentment, and anger towards the manager and the rest of the team that was not volunteered. The individual, at that point, can either get over it and move on or continue to hold the grudge. Holding on to grudges is not good for anybody and especially for the team, especially a team that is forming into a cohesive unit.

So why not go ahead and volunteer? The task has to be completed, anyway. Volunteer and have the task completed your way. Volunteering is a great way to stay visible (see Rule #10). More than likely the project/task is going to be viewed by other managers, supervisors, peers, and upper level leaders, then this is the perfect opportunity to be seen and to gain access to other members of the organization. Raising your hand and say you will do it, will certainly go a long way than being picked for the task.

Remember the piece of advice I mentioned earlier? "Never volunteer for anything"? We might need to change it a bit to just read "Volunteer". No matter what it is it has to be done. Remember, there are two types of tasks people are called on to volunteer for: Good and Bad. The Bad tasks are those that typically require you to get dirty, stinky and generally a mess. Think, washing out the trashcans, cleaning out the grease trap or any job that Mike Rowe considers a dirty job. Those jobs are not only necessary but they must be done, think about walking into a restaurant that has not cleaned out the grease trap in months. Yep, not a pretty scent and who would want to eat at a restaurant that smells like the rotting remains of everything they ever cooked?

On the other hand, there are the good tasks. The good tasks are usually the ones that involve some kind of labor (little, a lot, or none). The thing is for all tasks that require volunteers are all GOOD tasks. A few of those tasks will get messy and maybe a little stinky then again you might not. The point I am trying to make is there are NO good or bad tasks. There is only good or bad when it comes to performing the task. It is all about the attitude. Your attitude.

Whether you are "volunteered" or you volunteer to perform a task do it with enthusiasm. You have to give it your all. The trick here is to get the ones that assigned the task, in the first place, to see that not matter whether it is cleaning out the grease trap or spearheading the annual charitable contribution campaign, you are giving 100% of your attention, time, and effort. This is not the time to half-ass anything. If you do anything half-ass, one thing is certain you will find yourself being volunteered more often to wash trashcans and the like. Whatever you do end up doing, do it to 100% expectations and if you can, it is perfectly acceptable to exceed the expectations of the task you volunteered for or were volunteered to do.

Rule #12
Demand The Best From Your Superiors

Just like your supervisor, boss, and boss' boss will hold you accountable, you have every right and expectation to demand the best from them. They hired you because you were the best candidate for the job. You joined the organization or wanted to join the company because it was (and is) the best fit for you.

It was "quid pro quo" in its purest form. They did for you and you do for them. You work for the company and the company pays you. However, they also expect you to do your best. That is why you should also expect nothing but the best from your superiors.

It is like this: If you want to continue working at the place you like then know you will be expected to do the very best job that you can. If you like what you are doing and where you are working then it is safe to say you are wanting to stay where you work.

Then again, they want you to stay in a position of you giving them more than what they give you. The company does this by giving you a paycheck, bonuses, perks, and what they can. There are organizations that cannot give bonuses but they do give some leniency when it comes to taking time off, calling in sick and so on. The company is trading one type of benefit for another. In tough economic times, the organization must do what it can with the little it does have.

So where does demanding the best from the superiors come in? After all, they are being flexible, they are giving you a paycheck surely what more can they offer? What they can offer is keeping you informed by keeping you in the loop. They can also show you they support you and have your back when things do not go the way they were supposed to. Your superiors, supervisors, and company top management can also do something that is consider extra special. They can mentor you, whether you have already found a mentor as mentioned in RULE #8 (GET A MENTOR).

Mentoring is a "powerful personal development and empowerment tool. It is an effective way of helping

65

people to progress in their careers and is becoming increasing popular as its potential is realized. It is a partnership between two people (mentor and mentee) normally working in a similar field or sharing similar experiences. It is a helpful relationship based upon mutual trust and respect." (MentorSET,2008)

Ideally, you would want your immediate supervisor to be your mentor. However, some organizations have mentors that are from other departments or higher up the corporate ladder. This creates a broad based level of training and guidance. It also helps to create a well-rounded individual. Any organization is greatly enhanced by having well-versed individuals on the company rolls. The company instantly becomes better. The managers become better leaders. The employees become rooted in the corporate culture. That means you will like where you work because someone took the time to show you and give you the best they could offer.

A WORD OF WARNING: If your position has you taking more and more and giving less or delivering the minimum required the company allows. Guess what? You are wrong. Doing more will go a long way towards your superiors giving you more thus you will not have to demand as much as it is already being given. However, do not get Greedy! It is fine to demand more from your company but by the same token do not demand too much. When you demand too much you will come off as not satisfied with the company and the job you are doing. You will also give off the impression you are cocky and the company cannot live without you. Guess what? It was living before you and it will continue to exist long after your departure. Keep your demands in check.

Rule #13
You Are Not A Spy

If Rule number 13 sounds familiar well it should sound familiar. This rule is a carryover from "The Walking Leader" and applies to followers as it applies to leaders. In "The Walking Leader" I mention there will be some resistance and people will be suspect of your true intentions. I also mentioned it is important to ensure everyone knows the Walking Leader is not out there as a spy. It is almost as if, the Walking Leader has to go out of his way to ensure not to be perceived as a spy.

How does not being a spy apply you?

It applies in the sense you are out there meeting new people as well and you are out there to be a visible member of the organization. To be considered an "up and comer". To be someone that is a rising star within the company means others will become suspect of you and your true intentions. It is to be expected. It is when you others are not suspect of your or your intentions that you should start to worry.

You should worry because either you are not making yourself clear or no one is taking you seriously or seriously enough to bother you. All three, are signs of trouble. Trouble in the sense you are not doing what you need to be doing to be taken seriously. Everybody wants to be taken seriously everybody wants to be a contributing member of the team and there is nothing wrong with that. However, here is where it gets tricky. You might not be recognized because you are not making your intentions clear. Therefore, you have to be careful if you overdo it, when it comes to trying to tell people you are not a spy, you most certainly will come across as a spy.

However, spying for who?

Spying for your boss? Spying for the CEO? Or spying for yourself to get dirt on other people? You know what your intentions are, you know you are not spying and most certainly, you know no one put you up to this. Thus, it is important for you to not worry much if others become suspect of you and your intentions. After all, you are just trying to be a better follower and to be a better

69

follower you really need to know what is going on in the organization (within reason).

Therefore, you are spying for no one.

Of course, there will come a time when your supervisor or some other supervisor will corner you and accuse you of being a spy. What then? What can you do? You tell the truth is what you do!

It might not be what people want to hear but it is the truth. Even then, they still might not believe you. That is OK. You just have to show them.

By showing them, I mean, you keep doing what you have been doing. Now, is not the time to slack off or stop. As long as you are not breaking any company policies and procedures, you are fine! Of course, there will be a few that do not believe you and are hell bent on the fact you are spying on them, the department, and all the employees of the organization. Knowing fully well your intentions are true and above board, you just have to put up with it until others start buying into what you are doing.

The reality may be there will always be someone that will be suspect of you and of your intentions. As I wrote, you have to let them be. The more you put your foot down, the more they will believe you have something to hide. Then they know they got you, they really have you. Again, do not let it discourage you. Who knows it may be them that have something to hide?

There are people (think politicians) that will do everything they can to out an adversary. They will go out of their way to ensure the public knows every little dirty secret the opponent has ever attempted to hide. This is just a smoke screen. What the politician does not want you to know is that she has something to hide. The same applies in this case, while your intentions are honorable and true there will be those that have something to hide and will stop at nothing to ensure that what they have to hide stays hidden.

Think about this, if you just want to meet new people and work with everyone in the organization then it should be no problem to do just that. Now, you come across a certain individual and see him or her as a person you want to get to know. You introduce yourself and things start to develop. It is at this point, you become aware the individual is up to no good. Now you are in a position to expose that person. It would be unethical to not share what you know with your superior or the Human Resources department, however, the individual asks you not to rat him out. What then?

You are put between a rock and a hard place. You now know that you have to do what you did not set out to do. You become a spy. You struggle with the issue of violating a confidence and violating your moral and belief system.

Truth be told there is no struggle. There is no ethical dilemma. There is only you doing what you have to do. What you must do. That's it!

It is because you are not a spy that you can quickly report what is wrong. It is because you are not a spy that you continue being true to who you are and in turn you will be true to those around you, whether they are up to no good or not.

Plain and simple you are not a spy. You are not trained to be one. Well, unless you work for the CIA, KGB or MI6 then I thank you for your service and for taking the time to read this book. For the majority of us, we are just everyday people doing our everyday job but with something different, we want to be better than we were yesterday.

Rule #14
Take That Extra Step

At the end of Rule #11 (VOLUNTEER BUT DON'T LOOK LIKE YOU ARE VOLUNTEERING (a.k.a. Be A Helper)) I mentioned if you can it is perfectly acceptable to exceed the expectations of your assigned task. Now, I want to take this one-step further. How about always exceeding those expectations? What I mean, is if you are already doing your job to the best of your abilities how about finding one thing more that can make it better? For example, break down statistical data into a chart or graph then find and explain an angle that was previously not presented. Think outside the box but not so much that you spend more time explaining the extra bit than what the extra itself represents. I hope you get the picture. If not, that is OK, please read on there is more to come.

The first thing to remember when taking that extra step is you do not have to ask for permission to take the extra step. First, no one is going to give you permission. Not your supervisor, not your manager, not your supervisor's supervisor, and most certainly not your peers. This is not to make them out to be mean misers of doing what is right. The thing is if they give you permission, they will give you conditional permission. Conditional in the sense they will want you to do it their way. Is that really, what you want to do? I know it is not what you had in mind when you walked into the boss' office and asked for permission to do a little extra. It would break your heart; I know it would break my heart if I were told the only way I could take that extra step would be to take it their way.

You have to take the initiative. Plain and simple, there is nothing else to do, say, or ask. So long as that extra you plan on doing does nothing less than magic for you, your department, and your organization I would have to say you are good to go. If for some reason, what you perceive as "taking the extra step" or going above and beyond is nothing more than you just doing your job, then please STOP! Stop immediately. Do not pass "GO!" do not collect $200 just freeze in your tracks and stop.

You will really need to re-evaluate why what you think is above and beyond is nothing more than

"MEETING EXPECTATIONS" on your upcoming annual performance evaluation. Do not fall into the mindset that has many unfortunate souls believing that just showing up for work is a cause for fireworks celebration every hour on the hour. Remember, crossing the T's and dotting the I's is your job. In the current economy, there is NO room for individuals that allow mediocrity to drive their work ethic. In simpler terms, if you believe just showing up for work means you deserve a pay raise you will find out two things real quickly: you will find yourself looking for another job and there will be at least seven (if not more) individuals ready to fill your recently vacated position.

Now, if you believe taking the extra step means more than just 9 to 5 or a 40-hour workweek then you are on to something. If you are not sure as to what I am talking about, think about the following: someone approaches you for directions to an obscure office in your building. You know where the office is and you proceed to tell them how to get there. OK, it is your job to be courteous and tell them where to go and how to get there. You can take that a step further by drawing an accurate map. Better still, if you can walk with them to their destination or if you can call ahead and ask a co-worker to meet them at the elevator. It does not take much to go above and beyond but when you do people will remember you. When people remember you and your actions good things happen.

Here is something else. When there is a customer or client waiting for a co-worker to arrive and they are standing there looking uncomfortable go ahead and engage them. First, introduce yourself and ask them if they have been helped. More than likely the answer will be yes and they might tell you why they are waiting or whom they are waiting for. At this point, you can either check on what is keeping the person they are waiting for or you can engage them in light conversation or work on helping them yourself.

If you see someone that visibly needs help (help opening the door, carrying packages, etc.) then get up from your desk, walk over, and offer a helping hand. Do not wait until they are almost at arm's length from you to offer help. Seriously, at that point why bother? Trust me on this one, the moment you see someone needing help such as someone carrying a heavy load that requires two hands then get up, either open the door and then lighten their load or just lighten their load as soon as possible. Something to remember, it has been my experience, people do not refuse help when it is being offered especially when they are carrying a heavy load. Go ahead and offer that help. Now, if they absolutely refuse your help (lightening the load), stick close by just in case.

When the time comes and it will come, there will be individuals that will look at you with a sense of negativity. For whatever reason you will most certainly encounter, one or a few that are going to give you nothing but static and negativity. You can chalk their negativity to jealousy, envy, or they wish they had come up with the idea you are putting into action first.

It is not that difficult to go the extra mile, all you really need to do is go ahead take the extra step and go above and beyond. What is difficult is remembering to do it all the time, if you are not already doing it. What else will be difficult; will be those that see you as a "suck up" or whatever they want to see you as good or bad. That is fine, you cannot change their mind by saying anything. The only way to change their mind is to show them. Show them by taking the extra step and giving your stakeholders a little more than they originally expected is better for the organization, not just the individual. Do not get me wrong, the individual will most certainly benefit but giving the company some of the positive fallout does not hurt.

Rule #15
Know Your Co-Workers

There will come a time when you will need to work with co-workers that you have not met or even knew worked with the organization. This is one of those great opportunities to get to know those who work with you. Of course, most of us know the people in our department, section, or group but what about the people that work the overnight shift, seasonal employees or those located at remote offices? What about them? They are important members of the organization, as well. They are as critical to the success or the failure of the company as you are. Therefore, you should get to know them as well and you must do it now (not later).

Always extend a welcoming hand to everyone you encounter every day. Shaking someone's hand is a good way to build an almost instant bond. However, you must take care not to appear awkward; this is not your first handshake or is it? There are plenty of fantastic sources out there on how to shake someone's hand the right way.

If you are a handshaking veteran, it would not hurt to touch up on the proper etiquette of business handshakes. Consider it a great opportunity to hone your skills. Novice and veterans will put those skills to the test, every day. Once you get past the handshake, the rest is all downhill, well for the most part, it is downhill.

As you become familiar with your co-workers, you will have to determine what limits you want to have as you build a relationship with those individuals. You should go with your gut (or intuition) and set those limits early. A word or two of caution. Depending on what department assignment you have or what your role in the organization is, there will be individuals who will see you as their catalyst to fulfill a personal agenda or can make life easier for them. Then on the flipside do not assume that because you shake hands with someone in the organization's C-Level it means you have an automatic in at the top of the corporate food chain. Lastly, you should also be cognizant enough to know and understand there will be individuals that will be on the defense when it comes to any form of interaction. It would behoove you to be very careful with what you do and how you do it or you might find yourself standing in from of the desk of the

VP for Human Resources receiving a letter of reprimand for overstepping your boundaries. Please be very careful and trust yourself on how to proceed. Remember, no two individuals are alike and what might work for one might not work for someone else.

Once you have decided with whom your interactions will go beyond just a handshake then you can begin to get to know them on a more than just a professional level. However, you cannot skip past the professional level of getting to know a co-worker. Your first relationship with them will be working with them. You will have to know what they are capable and not capable of doing. You should know they are the right individuals for the job you will be calling on them to do. This makes it important to keep the non-professional interactions limited. There will be time for that later.

If a long-term approach is not something that appeals to you there are a few things, you can do now to get to know your co-workers. Asking to be assigned to a special project with co-workers you do not know or have never met is a great way to get to know others quickly. Think Jury Duty selection pool. Eventually, everyone that remains will form a bond. A small bond but a bond nonetheless.

Becoming a member of a special group or committee is a great way to increase your knowledge of your co-workers and their jobs within the organization. In addition, it is a great way to know who can do what, who to call on, and who will get the job done. Additionally, being assigned to a "special" group or committee creates a strong bond among the team members because they share a unique experience that was not available to the entire organization (again, think jury duty once selected). When the special project is complete, ask to be part of the next group that forms. Always keep your eyes and mind open to opportunities that arise and lead to meeting other members of the organization. However, always make certain you are doing your job before taking on any special projects because what good will the special project do your career if you cannot keep up with the work you were hired to do?

Once you get to know others in the organization and are prepared to escalate the relationship(s) to a non-professional, outside of work level be sure to keep it limited at first. The bottom line is you were co-workers first and the organization has to come first. What I mean is if you see the relationship might be heading down a dark path it may be best to put a halt to any further development and just keep the relationship at a professional, at-work level. It can be done without any hurt feelings. Remember, be honest and true to yourself, know what you want from the relationships, and be realistic when it comes to putting a stop to its development. Just remember to keep it real and the rest will be easy.

On the other side, if you decide to escalate the relationship outside of work there are a few important things to remember. Always try your hardest to keep the outside life on the outside. Did you notice I wrote, "try"? As we do not live in a perfect world, all we can do is try. Sure, some things will spill over to your work life and that is OK so long as things do not get out of hand and start affecting the performance of your job duties. Once your duties become affected rest assured you will be held accountable.

Pick your "outside of work" relationships wisely. You will encounter problems and successes along the way. When you encounter the bad times you will have to roll with the punches but also learn from them. Otherwise, you will repeat the bad over and over.

There is an old saying "never fish off the company pier." Guess what? This is very sound advice. Some people have taken this advice to heart ever since fishing off the company pier was frowned upon. Others have completely disregarded that advice to only find themselves on the losing twice, their relationship and their employment because the entire situation became a distraction. Then again, since the advent of the social media age the company pier has become a place where employees, customers, fans, and other stakeholders enjoy the fish fry, the lines of relationships can become very blurred. However, remaining adults throughout the entire situation and proceeding with caution, things will work out. Reverting to childish behavior when dealing with workplace relationships please be prepared to suffer the consequences, all of them.

Rule #16
Share With Others

Again, another rule that is a carryover from the "Walking Leader". There are some rules that are timeless and span across all levels of leadership. Sharing with others is one rule that can make or break any leader or follower. While it might sound a little harsh, it is the truth. You must share with others and by sharing I mean you are expected to teach others, show them what they do not know, and expect them to teach you and show you. The ability to share is a key component to being a team player.

Being a team player is essential to any successful career with any organization. Of course, I am not telling you anything new. I am simply re-affirming in the 21st Century work is all about teamwork and each member of the team is expected to deliver everything they can to the team in order for it to be successful in achieving its goal or mission. Team members are there for each other. Nothing turns a team inside out more than having someone, on the team, who is NOT a team player. When one refuses to be an active participant of the team, group, department or organization that individual is either looking for a way out or looking to be escorted from the premises. Active team members will see the individual that is not performing as someone who is not able to deliver when it comes to fulfilling the needs of the few or the many. Principally, the needs of the team.

Active team members will be those individuals that are not afraid to contribute, not afraid to lay it all on the line, the good and the bad, everything. That is what being a true team member is about. A true member of any team delivers the positive and the negative, even if it stings. How else can a team grow? How can it get better? How can any team or organization be a better group if no one is willing to offer the truth even if it is bad? There are plenty of opportunities to make a team better. However, there has to be someone there to exploit those opportunities. Sharing with others is the greatest way I know to exploit any opportunity.

When it comes to sharing with others, we must recognize not everyone knows everything. For example, members of the company's accounting department might not know what OSIP means. This is why everyone must share and share well. Of course, I am not talking about training an accountant to be a civil engineer but I am advocating for someone to help the accounting department when it comes to putting items of an engineering project in their proper place in the chart of accounts. By the way, OSIP stands for Operating Systems Implementation Plan. Then again, on the other side I would expect the accounting department to inform the engineering group what exactly the chart of accounts is and why it is fiscally important to the organization. Is that too much to ask for? NO!

Why is it so important to share information? Keeping all team members informed is essential to building a strong and cohesive team. When everyone knows what is going on, things get done. Magic can and does happen. Magic is made because well-informed decisions are taking place because of the information that is being shared. Sharing with others ensures all members of the team can count on each other and creates a level of real trust because everyone expects to be informed. The more you can do your part to create magic then the better off your team will be. Think about the following: imagine how ROCKING your team will be if every member is contributing on a constant and consistent basis. It would be "magical" would it not? It has to begin with taking the initiative and starting the conversation. Someone has to be the first to share, to communicate, let it be you.

The communication that is taking place must be a dialogue when sharing occurs. The dialogue is expected as everyone is not only sharing information but also providing feedback, asking questions and critiquing throughout the entire dialogue. Sharing with others minimizes monologues. The monologues do not give any real substance to the information being shared other than just the facts. Be careful not to share too much in the form of monologues, as others will start to expect the same from you. Remember, monologue never have and never will be dialogue.

Do not get me wrong, monologues have their place in business. However, you should seek out every opportunity to move from monologues to dialogues. Encourage others to share what they know or what they are thinking. Especially, if what they are thinking about is relevant to you or your team's ongoing operations. The exchange of information is expected, after all, that is what true sharing is all about?

Now, do not start a dialogue or continue one for the sake of starting one or continuing one. As I wrote, there will be times when monologues are OK. Pick the conversation and move on. Listen to the person presenting the initial information then go from there. It is easy to continue the conversation when the individual asks if anyone has any questions or comments. However, there will be times when there is no need for comment. When you are sharing information with others, go with your gut on whether you want feedback or not. Otherwise, keep sharing and do it often throughout the process.

Do not be afraid to get out there and share with everyone. Take it at your own pace and understand when it comes to sharing, your leaders should be setting the example, especially when you are new to the workplace. When you share with others your managers and leaders will recognize you are committed to making the team better. They will also get firsthand experience on what you are made of and what you bring to the company buffet (more on that later).

Now, if your leaders and managers are NOT setting the example what then? If you are new to the team do not worry (just yet). Give yourself time to get to know how the team does business and then dive in. However, if you have been there a while then there is absolutely no excuse for your lack of sharing. Start sharing right now. Do not worry about finishing the rest of this book, just start now. If you really need your supervisor's permission to start sharing with your teammates and throughout the organization then it may be time to ask yourself if are you really where you want to be? If people are making it nearly impossible to share with others then there is something wrong going on and you should ask yourself again, is this a place you really want to be? Otherwise, GET OUT THERE, START SHARING AND MAKE MAGIC HAPPEN NOW (not later)!

Rule #17
Evaluate Yourself, Constantly

You will find that "evaluating yourself constantly" will be the most difficult of all the rules in the entire WALKING LEADER trilogy. As you go from follower to leader, your supervisors and their supervisors will constantly evaluate you. You and your actions will be scrutinized every time, all the time. It would make sense to be on the offense and start evaluating yourself constantly. This in no way means you should develop some kind of inferiority complex but it does mean to become aware of yourself, what you are doing, and what you are trying to do. By all means, you are expected to be critical of yourself. Famous Chinese philosopher, Lao Tzu, said, "He who knows others is wise; he who knows himself is enlightened" and famous playwright William Shakespeare in the tragic play Hamlet wrote, "To thine own self be true, and it must follow, as the night the day, thou canst not then be false to any man." Both men wrote these words centuries apart yet they both knew the importance of knowing yourself.

It is in knowing yourself that you can truly measure what you have done, what you are doing and what you are capable of doing. Therefore, the ability to evaluate yourself means you are taking your role as an employee of the organization as seriously as possible. It also means you recognize the fact that you can always do better, no matter what your role is in the organization, you can always do better as can your peers.

Your peers are an excellent resource when it comes to providing feedback about your performance, attitude, and goals. A word of caution, pick those individuals that are not afraid to tell you the truth but also do not believe you are just being a suck-up or ass-kisser. Those that say you are only doing this is to become a suck-up are bringing their own agenda to the table and will never give you an honest response or feedback. While that is unfortunate, it also lets you know whom you can count on and whom you cannot. Do not be afraid of the responses or answers others may or may not give when you ask them to give you feedback. If they can handle providing constructive feedback then you can handle it, even if it is not in your favor. You know what you can do with those that bring petty jealousy into the feedback they provide, take it with a grain of salt. However, be careful to ensure you are not surrounding yourself with "yes" men and women.

If at some point you are getting more positive feedback than negative, you should be concerned that something is not quite right. It is time to start questioning the feedback to make sure it has not become expected and disconnected. If all you continue to get is only positive feedback it may be time to bring in other peers to get a "fresh pair of eyes" on the situation and you now have feedback that's less tainted and fresh.

Another great source to provide you with unobscured feedback is from your supervisors. Yes, supervisors are a great resource for providing feedback. I have discovered supervisors are apt to give you feedback when you approach them first. It seems most supervisors would rather dispense feedback long before they are forced to do so during the annual review. By genuinely starting now, you put yourself in a situation in which you and your supervisor work to develop and implement a plan of action long before your next annual performance review. Speaking of annual performance review, a good by-product of soliciting feedback from your supervisor is that your supervisor retains more of the good stuff you have done over the past year and less of the bad as you are already working to improve yourself.

You might also consider soliciting feedback from your supervisor's supervisor. This could come in handy when the time comes to replace your supervisor. I am not advocating a bloody coup but what I am advocating is to be prepared for when your supervisor leaves his current position either because of a promotion, a higher paying job somewhere else, or retirement as that position will need to be filled. Why not you? Who is better to fill your boss' vacated shoes? You! Pick your time wisely and be sure to let your supervisor know what you want to do before you approach your boss' boss. It might help if you can get your supervisor to introduce you to his supervisor.

Once you have settled in and accepted that self-evaluation will be part of your professional routine you can then proceed to build on the foundation you have created. The first thing to do is to determine how you want to evaluate yourself. Will you do it solely on professional accomplishments, relationships, both, or something completely different? Get that locked down and you can then start self-assessing and processing to your heart's content.

Once you have your self-evaluation method under control, you will have to orient yourself to decide and act on what you want to work on and accomplish to be a better employee. Thus, you will have to develop your own action plan to improve. This action plan does not have to be completed. You can use your collected data to determine where you stand and what you need to work on. Put the plan in writing. Remember, if it is not in writing it is not real.

If it is not real then how can you achieve the goals you want to accomplish based on your action plan? It really is that simple. Just put it in writing, for Pete's sake. Once it is in writing, you can start setting very realistic goals and a realistic period in which to achieve those goals. Be realistic, I mean you should not plan to complete the goals in your action plan all at the same time or as quickly as possible. Remember, it took a lifetime to get you to this point in your life. Take it easy when it comes to setting a schedule towards reaching your goals or determining your goals for that matter. Once everything is set and you are executing your action plan be sure to take time to revisit what you are doing, why you are doing it, and what you can do to do it better.

You can revisit your action plan daily, every other day or at least weekly. Take a 360° degree look around at how things are progressing and make subtle changes as you go along. Those subtle changes will yield big results later. If you are not too sure how to take the time to review all you have to do then find a quiet spot, pull out your written action plan and see where you are, either forward or backward, from the same time the previous week. Keep it simple. There is no guarantee you will be successful but I can guarantee you will start to learn more about yourself. In learning more about yourself through honest and realistic self-assessments, you start to become confident in your abilities, capabilities, and limitations. Once you get confident in that, you can start to grow and become better than you were when your first started evaluating yourself.

Rule #18
Bring More To The Company Buffet
Than Just Your Appetite

Bringing more to the company buffet than just your appetite means you are doing what it takes to bring value to the company and not some "mindless" cog in the corporate wheel collecting a paycheck. You have to be prepared to do what it takes to ensure the return on the investment your company has already committed to you and your training will yield more than just what they have already put in. You had better be refilling the company coffers otherwise do not be surprised when the time comes you find yourself by yourself and out of a job.

I know this may sound harsh but you have to understand these are harsh times. These are times that people cannot afford to let slip away. Your company has internal and external stakeholders to report to and when times are tough everyone is going to ask the tough questions and they are going to expect the brutal, HONEST truth. If you are one of those individuals that is constantly, filling your plate and not giving back then prepare yourself for the worst.

How can you tell you if you are one of those individuals? It is very simple, if you have to ask yourself if you are one of those individuals, then you most certainly are. I suggest you start clearing out your desk because your walking papers are not too far behind.

However, there is hope. When you realize you are filling your plate but returning little to no value, it may or may not already be too late. Think about this, not next week, right now; start every work day thinking about the value you will be bringing to the company today and deliver on that. At the end of every workday do a healthy self-assessment of what you did bring that was of value to the company today. If you find that you bring in more value than what you are putting on your plate then you are good to go. However, if what you bring in is not even close to what are you pilfering from the organization then you better start ramping things up a notch or two (or three) otherwise, you will be shown your way out.

Seriously, you need to start looking deep and hard at how much value (monetary and otherwise) to the company you are bringing. You should also consider starting right now at improving the amount of value you bring. Whether it be writing code, answering customer support calls, or processing invoices, it does not matter what you do, what matters is the quality and not the quantity. Anyone can answer the telephone 500 times in an eight-hour workday but if quality is not associated with those customer support calls then what is the point? If all you did is manage to infuriate 500 callers then you did NOTHING positive for the company brand. Remember, if one caller has a bad experience they will tell 20 people and with 500 infuriated callers that can come out to 10,000 people, in no time, that now know about your organization's bad customer service. Your organization? Yes, your organization those 500 callers called for support and while they more than likely will not remember your name or operator number. What they will remember is that it was your company they were calling. I hope you get the picture.

Now, if you can answer half those calls and turn them all into very satisfied customers, you just made magic happen. Do something to make their experience memorable (refer to Rule #14 "Take the extra step" if you need guidance with this). Make them take notice about just how much you and your organization truly cares. Do that and you are most definitely giving more back to the organization. Then people will really start to take notice of you and the good you are doing for the company and for yourself.

When the quality of the work improves your manager or supervisor will notice. They will notice because the people above will also notice. The same goes when performance and quality degrades. Your supervisor and your supervisor's supervisor will ask what are you doing or what happened to either increase or decrease the quality of your work. They will ask so they can figure out how to replicate or prevent it from happening throughout the department or company. Trust me; you would rather be the one responsible for positive change throughout the company than becoming a cautionary tale at the next company retreat. Bringing value means increasing quality and not quantity, so bring it. Otherwise, why bother working for the organization? Look at and focus on improving quality instead of quantity. Take care of quality and the quantity will take care of itself.

As always, if you find yourself needing help on how to bring more to the company buffet all you have to do is ask somebody. Start with your supervisor or a mentor; ask someone who you feel comfortable asking. Maybe by taking the initiative and asking for help you might have saved yourself from the company chopping block.

The last take away is to always remember and never ever forget the Company Buffet is a Potluck.

Rule #19
Be Patient

"Patience is bitter, but its fruit is sweet." -Aristotle

When it comes to being a great follower, a great leader, a great boss, a great business owner you cannot expect it to happen in a hurry. It being recognition, reward or advancement. You must be patient. I know no one wants to hear the words: Be Patient. Easier said than done, right? Unfortunately, there is no shortcut to be a great follower or a great leader. You have to pay your dues. Everyone before you did it and everyone after you will do it. They and you have no choice, it is just the way it is, it is the way it has always been, it will always be this way and there are no shortcuts to take to make it happen without paying your dues.

Paying your dues means you are in it for the long haul. You cannot half-ass your approach or commitment to becoming better than what you are. If you half-ass it, achieving greatness will not take you twice as long, you just will not achieve it at all. Paying your dues means you have to work for yourself to promote yourself. You will have to be careful that you do not come off as too cocky, too arrogant, or too full of yourself. Just be yourself. By putting in the hard work and learning your craft, you will be well on your way to greatness. It will not be an overnight trip. The journey may be long, cold and arduous but to get to where you want to go you still have to take that road. It is going to be a long and bumpy road but you can make it.

While you are on your way, there may come a time when you are recognized for the hard work you are putting in or for the skill(s) you are demonstrating in your craft and that is fantastic. While you have caught someone's attention now you have to do all you can to keep it. However, never rest on your laurels because you are far from making it. There are people that see a little sign of life and think (no, they assume) they have made it. Nothing could be further from the truth. They are the ones that will rest on their laurels only to have their feet kicked out from underneath them. They then have to struggle that much more to get to back to the initial level of recognition. Hopefully, they will remember to keep moving onward and upward otherwise they will enter a cycle climbing up the mountain then falling down that mountain and repeating that because they make same mistake again. They may never break out of that cycle. Do not get caught up in any of that. Those that spotted you will quickly move on to the next person that shows signs of life quicker than refreshing your Twitter feed.

Every organization expects its leaders to find those diamonds in the rough, those hidden gems. When they find those diamonds in the rough, the leader is then expected to acknowledge them and see if they can polish that "diamond" into something that becomes an asset. If your leader gives you recognition do not let any of that recognition go to your head. Stay focused and stay the course. Remember, being on their radar does not mean the key to the executive washroom is one pat on the back away. Any recognition you receive you will accept with a heartfelt "thank you" but that is all you should do other than keep doing what you have always done and moving forward. Keep working and above all keep improving. Do that and before you know it, your recognition will turn into appreciation and then into advancement.

Advancement within the organization is not without its own caveats. Advancement may be long in coming and might actually be the purest form of being patient. Advancement in any organization is typically not dispensed on a regular basis. The military, state agencies, and in the private sector all have that in common. Sure, there are some "career ladders" but for the most part, most organizations have built-in objectives that must be met before anyone can be considered for promotion.

This is where patience is critical. Think about the following: A Second Lieutenant in the US Army will typically see the junior enlisted men, under his command, promoted once, twice, or even three times before the Lieutenant sees his own promotion to First Lieutenant. Talk about being patient. That is also the case in the private and public sectors. Senior staff may go years without a promotion or even a pay raise, in favor of ensuring the lower level staff get something. An organization that would just as soon give pay raises to the members of the top before paying the ones on the frontlines is an organization that is setting a very bad example for its followers and future leaders. It is also an organization does not have a future.

Of course, there will be times you will have to wait a long time before any formal recognition comes your way. If available, take advantage of the company perks. They are there for a reason and they are there to be used. If there is criteria that has to be met by you or any employee before having access to the benefits then guess what? That is right, you have to be patient, meet the goals or objectives and be patient.

As humans, in the 21st Century, patience is not something we gravitate towards naturally. In all actuality, we hate it. We truly despise it. Everything around us is either instant on, always on, or never closes. Our phones encourage the disdain of patience. Our smartphones connect us to almost any place on the planet. A few finger swipes and before you can blink the time, temperature and weather forecast for Tegel Airport in Berlin, Germany appears on your handheld device.

No matter how you look at it, you have to keep doing your best and do it for as long as it takes. Then when the time comes, the reward of recognition and advancement will be well worth it. As I started this chapter with a quote from Aristotle, I felt it was the perfect quote for what you want when it comes to being a follower and a leader. Understand reward and advancement does not necessarily mean more money and corner office. Typically, it means being recognized for who you are and what you have become. It means people look to you for guidance. It also means people respect you and your opinion. It most certainly means you are a recognized leader. Now if they want to pay you and give you a corner office then never forget to say *"Please"* and *"Thank you"*.

Rule #20
Have Fun!

I have said it before and I will continue to say it, "If you are not having fun, why bother?" Seriously, there is nothing better when doing your job or going to work than having fun. However, you should be careful as to not have so much fun you start to neglect your duties. No matter how much fun you are having if your duties are being neglected rest assured you will soon find yourself having no fun at all. So all things in moderation.

In the current workplace environment, there is only so much room for fun. Sure there are companies like Google and Yahoo that have in-house masseuses and foosball tables on every floor of the company headquarters but most businesses wish they could provide just a quarter of what Google offers its employees. If you are working at Google and Yahoo, you know exactly what I am talking about. All that fun in those places of work. How does any real work ever get done? How can those two companies become two of the top internet companies on the planet? Simple. Their corporate culture is based on working hard and having fun.

Google, Yahoo, and others like them know there is a time and place for everything. Those companies and their employees know when to party and when to get to work. Those companies strive to go the extra mile to keep the employees focused and engaged. The bottom line here is they know what it takes to have fun and how to turn that fun into individuals that want to make those companies the best in the world while having fun.

The same can be for you. If you want to be part of the best organization in the world then it is up to you to do the best you can and not just for the company but for yourself. If you want to have fun, then it is up to you to have all the fun you can. Do not forget that. The same goes for being the best employee and it is up to you to be the best employee your company has ever known.

A fantastic by-product of having fun at work is fueling a creative mind. Having a creative mind leads to being innovative. It leads to innovation. Innovation is what has keeps companies like Google, Yahoo, and Cisco

Systems on top of their game. So what if you are not working for Google, Yahoo, Cisco, or Apple? You can still have fun. You can still be creative. You can be innovative and be a bigger, better asset to your organization.

Have Fun, otherwise why bother?

Seriously, if you find yourself lacking in the fun department when it comes to work you really need to look at why it is no longer fun or was it ever fun? Obviously, no one goes to work for an organization thinking they will not have fun working there. Most people truly believe fun can be had at almost any job. It is sad but there are few that cannot find the fun in what they are doing. Unfortunately, they are also the loudest individuals you will hear in the organization. It has been my experience, those that cannot find the fun in what they are doing, cannot find it because they are doing a job they are not prepared to do.

They are not prepared to do the job either because of lack of education or experience. They just cannot effectively do the job and it shows. Thus, they become loud, obnoxious and find fault in others in hopes that they, themselves, will not get found out. If you find yourself in

111

this situation, there is nothing wrong with admitting what you lack and move on. Do not think of this as defeat. When you realize you are way over your head and want to "stop the madness" then say so. Admitting you need help is not defeat, it is actually a winning mindset, in that you recognize the company is a team and the members of the team must work together to be better, to be successful, and to be fun. Remember, it is actually considered a success when you can identify the problem, determine a solution, and then act on that solution.

Who knows, you might find the fun you were missing is somewhere else within your current organization. Then again, if finding and having fun takes you to where you will be an asset for a different company then you will leave the current organization much happier than when you were there.

Do not be afraid to have fun. Have fun, no matter where you are and no matter what you do. Take a chance at having fun in a different location, if you have to. However, do not settle on doing something you are not having fun doing. Never settle for that! If you are just going through the motions and being miserable (or not having fun), imagine just how successful you will be when you are at your happiest.

Have Fun!

Rule #21
(Bonus) Work Is To Stay At Work &
Home Is To Stay At Home

Something can be said about the individual that can leave WORK at WORK when the whistle blows at 5 o'clock and can leave HOME at HOME when the whistle blows to start the workday.

Imagine being able to turn off all your "at home" worries and solely focus on the work at hand: your job.

Imagine being able to turn off all the day's events and have a restful, peaceful evening at home with your family?

Some say because of the age we live in, the ALWAYS ON, ALWAYS CONNECTED, 24/7 world we cannot break the electronic chains that bind us to work, in the evening. For the same reason, we cannot break those digital chains that tie us to family during the day. The stress of always being connected makes it essential to have a place where you can go to escape the workplace.

To minimize the stress at home, make all or part of your home a WORK FREE ZONE (WFZ). The WFZ is where you will not check your work email every half hour. You will not do work from work for the sake of doing work from work. You will not answer your work phone because it is ringing. Guess what? That is why voicemail was created and that is why people play "phone tag", so let the call go to voicemail and get back with them later or better yet, first thing in the morning.

Remember, if the caller does not understand why you did not answer the phone on the first ring, then they truly do not respect what you stand for, your time off from work, and most of all, they do NOT respect you. Then, it might be time to rethink that relationship, especially if the person not respecting your time off is your boss.

As for "Home is to Stay at Home" the other side of the "Work is to Stay at Work" this may be the most difficult to do. See when you were hired, you were hired to do a job for your employer who would in turn give you compensation for doing that job. However, the reality is

115

that many of us bring our home into the workplace and are not really doing the job we are paid to do.

The kids call with a homework question, the wife calls to remind you to pick up milk and bread on the way home or your significant other calls to make plans on where to meet for dinner. It is going to happen and nothing is going to change that. However, you should do everything within your power to curtail the number of interruptions "from home". Any attempt to restrict the outside calls from your friends and family while on company time should be as honest and sincere as possible. Otherwise, why bother?

As the economy continues to improve, everyone must do more with less and your employer is going to expect you to do more of your job and less socializing, that means less time spent off the job when you are supposed to be on the job. This might sound harsh but understand in an economy that is still taking no prisoners there is no room for slacking off or the perception of slacking off and goofing off on company time. That is why you must enlist the help of your friends and family to get them to support you in keeping the calls and distractions down to a minimum.

Emergencies are understandable and expected. Emergencies are an acceptable part of be life but living in a constant state of emergency is certainly not understandable and definitely NOT expected nor tolerated by the employer (any employer). Do what you can now to limit the outside distractions otherwise it may be too late.

The same goes for keeping work at work. Your family and friends will want you to be present when you are with them. Make it a point to be with them every chance you get. Once those opportunities are gone, they are gone forever. Take advantage of all the "at home" time you can.

It may be tricky to navigate between the two lives (work and home) but it can be done. No, it MUST be done. There will be times when one life will have to sacrifice itself for the other. So long as it does not become a permanent sacrifice then everything should be fine when balance and order is restored. Returning to a balanced work-home life the sooner the better will be good for both worlds. Keep working hard to keep both lives in order and everything will pay off in the end.

Now, get back to work.

References

BIBLIOGRAPHY

Coleman, J. (2013, May 13). Six Components of a Great Corporate Culture. Harvard Business Review. Retrieved July 11, 2014, from http://blogs.hbr.org/2013/05/six-components-of-culture/

Marcus, B. (2014, JANUARY 06). Advice from top women leaders about finding a mentor. Retrieved from http://www.forbes.com/sites/bonniemarcus/2014/01/06/advice-from-women-leaders-about-finding-a-mentor/

Reber, P. (2010, APRIL 19). What is the memory capacity of the human brain?. Retrieved from http://www.scientificamerican.com/article.cfm?id=what-is-the-memory-capacity

What is Mentoring?. (2008, January 1). . Retrieved May 17, 2014, from http://www.mentorset.org.uk/pages/mentoring.htm

About The Author

David Guerra is a former active duty US Army Infantryman and comes from a long line of US Army Soldiers. His first assignment was right in the center of the Cold War: West Berlin. Serving in West Berlin certainly made an impact on David's view of the world. His views on personal and professional growth were heavily influenced by what he experienced while assigned 110 miles behind the Iron Curtain.

Since leaving the US Army, David spent 17 years working for the State of Texas and now works in the Private Sector. Along the way, he successfully earned his BBA and an MBA.

In 2013, David published his first business leadership book, "The Walking Leader", as the first in a planned trilogy of leadership books. The last book, "We, The Team" is expected to be completed and available in 2016.

David is also the author of the OCCUPIED BERLIN book series.

You can find David online just about any time:

- twitter.com: @daveguerra

- email: dave@daveguerra.com

- web: http://www.daveguerra.com

- facebook: http://www.facebook.com/thedavidguerra

- linkedin:

http://www.linkedin.com/profile/view?id=1095097

- web: http://www.berlinbrigade.com